A MESSAGE IN A BOTTLE

A WALK WITH FAITH

DARREN TERELL JACKSON

A MESSAGE IN A BOTTLE
Copyright © 2022 **Darren Terell Jackson**

All rights reserved. No part of this book may be used or reproduced by any means, graphic, electronic, or mechanical, including photocopying, recording, taping or by information storage and retrieval system without the written permission of the author except in the case of brief quotations embodied in critical articles and reviews.

Stratton Press Publishing
831 N Tatnall Street Suite M #188,
Wilmington, DE 19801
www.stratton-press.com
1-888-323-7009

Because of the dynamic nature of the Internet, any web addresses or links contained in this book may have changed since publication and may no longer be valid. The views expressed in the work are solely those of the author and do not necessarily reflect the views of the publisher, and the publisher hereby disclaims any responsibility for them.

Any people depicted in stock imagery provided by Shutterstock are models, and such images are being used for illustrative purposes only.

ISBN (Paperback): 978-1-64895-735-2
ISBN (Hardback): 978-1-64895-737-6
ISBN (Ebook): 978-1-64895-736-9

Printed in the United States of America

Have you ever gone walking on a secluded white sandy beach somewhere in the tropics fantasizing about finding a bottle with a note in it?

Well, I do all of the time. I think about finding a letter with the confessions from a hopeless romantic or if it will contain a map to a hidden treasure that will enrich my life forever like an *epiphany*.

In my dreamy state of mind on a tantalizing summer morning, this particular bottle with an odd globe-like top and a mysteriously small book inside of it washed upon the shoreline as I was unpacking my fishing gear anticipating a trophy-sized catch.

I could clearly read the words "In God We Trust" and this weird symbol with the words "Asase Ye Duru" on its cover.

I shattered the bottle and began to indulge myself into what appears to be an intriguing way to a fulfilling life book. I was totally mesmerized while being led on an unfathomable journey loaded with heavenly sent messages and priceless wisdom.

I started learning so much about the meaning of life and its possibilities in our global existence; it still has my head spinning. That is why I created this painting titled *The Metamorphosis*. It is a headshot of my reaction to another confirmation that all things are possible through Christ like when Sen. Barack Obama (first African American US president) was elected as the president of our United States of America against all odds. I must be dreaming!

I never lacked any self-confidence, but that historic day made me feel proud to be an African American.

His amazing accomplishment became my spirited affirmation. Suddenly, I grew an inch taller because I held my head up high and just simply stood up straight with my chest pumped out. I went from being a soft-spoken introvert to having the audacity to become a multimedia expressionist; my brush strokes became more vibrant and purposely authoritative.

I thought that maybe my artworks would get fair recognition for their dynamic applications and for their meaningful contents.

After further reading in this jewel of a book, I found more hidden treasures. It was how prayer and meditation can change your life.

Applying those principles, such as organizing and prioritizing your desires, also opening up your mind to positive alternatives to cope with and relieve stress, have proven to be beneficial. That is why I created this painting titled *Meditation* as a symbol to remind me that praying with deep focus, then proceeding with great intentions can be very effective.

This overwhelming and nonsuperficial resource of information threw me for a loop. I had to take a step back to reevaluate my situation and the path I was on and also where that path would lead me… It occurred to me that I would have more of the same if I didn't change anything.

I did some soul-searching and dug deeper within my heart to rethink my goals and values. I needed to alter my life's trajectory.

I had to shut down everything around me to include my collective family, friends, social distractions, and even my curious neighbors next door. It took me some time to adjust, and when I did, a light came on.

Thanks to the incredible teachings from that book again, the road ahead appeared narrower, filled with less potholes, less sinkholes, fewer bad curves, and even the uphill climbs are smoother now.

I felt compelled to make a painting titled *The Inward Spiral* hoping it conveys the idea I want to share.

As my consciousness expanded beyond my personal space, a new series was born: The Faith Walk Series. The first painting is titled *Manifestations*, it depicts a figure in a fetal position after letting go of its beliefs to start a new beginning in a new world.

The second painting titled *The Awakening* depicts a person rotating on the highest peak with the ability to see all things after becoming enlightened by the mind-body-spirit concept.

The third painting titled *The Messenger* is an angelic figure walking about to and from spreading the gospel and sharing valuable information to those who will listen. I was always impressed with total strangers, who you would have never thought of, to have so much knowledge on a particular subject that can lead you in the right direction. That is why we should "never judge a book by its cover."

For example, I remember I would often see this scraggly old man in the cafeteria at Virginia Hospital Center in Arlington, Virginia. He was always accompanied with someone until one day there was only one available seat next to him, he just happened to be alone at the time. I asked him if the seat was taken and he replied, "No, young man, this seat is all yours, sit down and enjoy your lunch." I accepted his offer.

We introduced ourselves and started a remarkable conversation. He told me that he was retired, and now he's a pianist and he travels to many hospitals up and down the East Coast providing free performances. I looked at him and I said, "That's nice of you, but how is that possible?" He looked so poor and homeless. He told me that he is a very rich man, and he enjoys helping the sick and the needy. His kids are both professionals, one a doctor and the other a lawyer. He meets up with them from time to time at his beach house in Florida, so when he's not hanging out with them, he shares his blessings with others—not with money but with music, wise tales, and encouraging advice.

Being in this guy's presence was awesome. He is the reason why I treat all walks of life with the same courtesy and respect, because you never know how impactful someone can be for you in spite of their outward appearance. Mr. Tom was my angel in disguise.

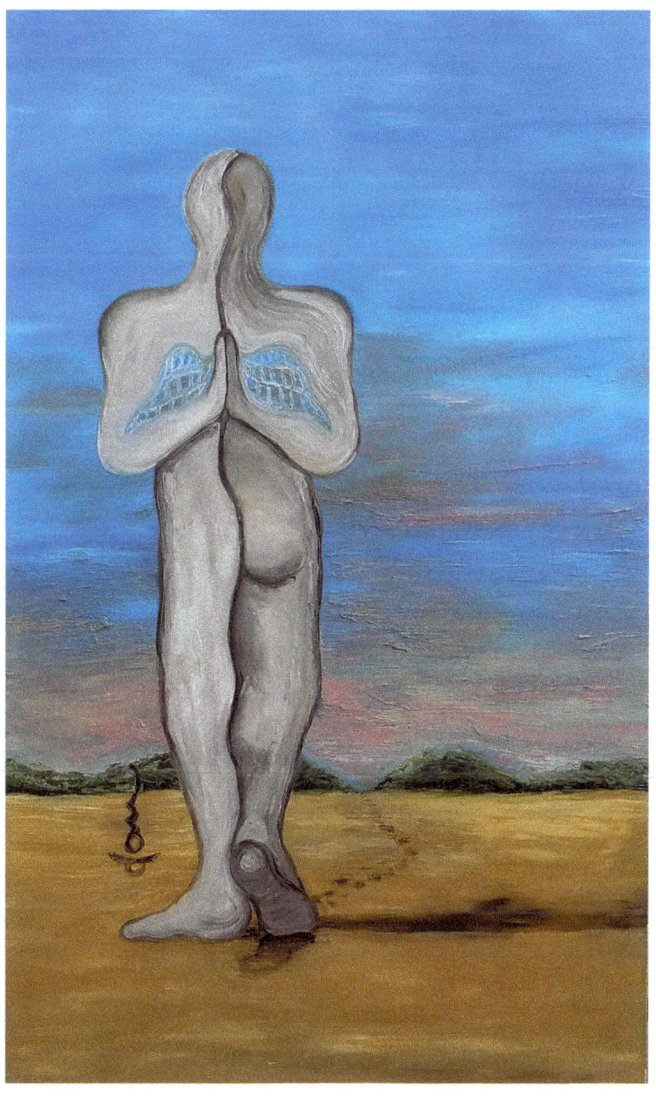

What is the definition of a soul mate? Well, my fourth painting portrays that answer as divine unity, a match made in heaven, and my life partner. It is definitely someone who compliments the other's weaknesses and strengths without stepping on any toes…wouldn't that be lovely?

My fourth painting is titled *The Rain Dancers*. It depicts a dancing couple unfazed by their negative surroundings because together their happy hearts beat indefinitely as one.

My fifth and final installment of The Faith Walk Series is titled *The Promise Fairy*, it was inspired by my fascination with orbs as a little kid.

My first introduction to this magical sensation was around the Christmas holiday season. My mother would shake this clear globe filled with snowflake-like crystals, and when everything settled down, Santa Claus appeared. That encounter filled me with pure joy. I am still moved by that element today.

I love to paint meaningful objects with ancient catchphrases inside of these cylinders that will exude the same sentiment.

The first orb contains the tree of life—a constant reminder that you are a soul connected to heaven and earth. The second orb contains an hourglass—time is a blessing, live freely and enjoy life in the moment. The third orb contains a moonlit path—follow your dreams, create your own path. The fourth orb contains a lotus flower—it is a symbol of rising out of suffering. The fifth orb is a cornucopia filled with figs—be a noble servant and reap the fruits of your labor. The sixth orb is a sunrise—the dawn of a new day, immortality, God's promise for eternal life.

Another chapter in the book reminds us to be grateful, especially for the simple things, because those are the secret jewels that our subconscious is looking for.

I believe that art is essential, art is perpetual, and art is infinite. I believe that the earth deserves more conservation. I also believe that we are here today and gone tomorrow. I believe that we all are a force of nature. I believe that life is what you make it so I am looking for this wonderful space, and when I find it, I will make it last forever.

That takes us to my next inspired painting and poem with the same title.

Finding Forever

A place where the stars align
A place where precious food is divine
A place where I stand as tall as a Baobab tree
A place where no matter where you are spiritually,
there is Love for you and me,
A place that has Salvation for those who come together
A place where having character is a treasure.

Do you know your purpose in life? That is the ultimate question to ask yourself. Does anyone really know the answer? I certainly do not have a clue, but what I do know is that I am cursed and blessed with creative energy. If I had the power to make a difference, I would like to impact the world with visual enlightenment and to encourage everyone to live life to their highest potential.

Not a minute goes by when I am not thinking about how I can create something beautiful and meaningful. This uncontrollable dynamic force has me completely *spellbound*.

Did you know that you can achieve escapism to a desired destination without costing you a penny? Have you heard of the word *staycation*? It is like taking a local affordable vacation getaway in the comforts of your own home.

Now just imagine having the legal and spiritual freedom to explore life as much as you can dream of.

I decorate a room or a whole house with the ambiance of destinations anywhere on the planet—in any city, in any country—by using the unique objects, fragrances, foods, music, clothing, and even the temperature of a destination because it provides an outlet from my current situation by releasing the confinements of structure and limitations. It is a magnificent psychological moment where I have no boundaries. This technique simulates an extraordinary space that is *uninhibited*.

When it rains, it pours. I was in the midst of my spring-cleaning regimen when I squatted down to pick up the dustpan, and for some reason, I could not stand back up. It was the most frightening time in my life. I managed to seek medical attention to find out what was wrong. After having an MRI exam, my neurologist told me that if I don't get emergency surgery right now, the alternative will be paralysis from the neck down.

Unfortunately, that head-and-neck injury I suffered a while ago came back to haunt me. My herniated cervical disc slowly degenerated to a point where they caused spinal cord compression and nerve entrapment. By the grace of God, I am still standing because my anterior cervical discectomy and fusion surgery was a success.

That's not it! Later on that year in the fall season that I love so dearly, I was headed home from work when a huge buck deer stepped out in front of me; and sadly, I destroyed it and totaled my truck. If that wasn't horrific enough, I had a relationship meltdown while being caught up in a pursuit for an oasis.

Our home, joy on the inside and joy on the outside.

A place of comfort, security, beauty, refuge, pride, and many blessings.

Oh, the joy and anxiety to find that special place turned out to be a complete heartbreak. So much turmoil within the transitioning of lifestyle differences, design ideas, and basic cohesion suffered tremendously.

This exciting journey for total unification turned into darkness, silence, and utter confusion.

Instead of a place filled with prosperity, I reached a place far from sublime.

My passion to seek fulfillment was overshadowed a different reality.

The other force in this dynamic relationship had a life pace that exploded in my face like a fall from grace.

I became overwhelmed with emotions with no rhyme, reason, or explanation, until a healing voice whispered to my *naked soul* to just keep striving with no hesitation.

Lessons Learned, Messages Received

> The Lord is near to all who call him, to all who call on him in truth. (Matt. 145:18)

> Thou shalt love thy neighbor as thyself. (Matt. 22:39)

True Confession

    Dear, Lord, I surrender to your will. Please forgive me for my sins. I shall resist my selfish temptations and halt where foolishness begins.

    I was ignorant to your light, now I see the power of your mercy, I'm grateful for another chance, to be a servant for thee.

    Thanks for a *new life*.

Chasing a dream is filled with hopes and desires; following a dream is a journey loaded with challenges beyond belief. In other words, making a commitment to follow a dream is an intense process of highs and lows.

The sacrifices that are necessary to stay the course includes first and foremost the means to afford the materials you need to start a hobby, business, or an activity. In most cases, you need a second income.

The next obstacle is finding the time to be creative. Life has so many demands on your time like having to work two jobs to make ends meet, raising kids, maintaining your household from breakdowns, it requires reliable transportation, taking care of your health, and if you have a spouse, you must share yourself physically and emotionally. I am sure that there are many more distractions to keep you preoccupied from discovering your true potential.

The third thing is, I strongly believe for success you are going to need help, not just any support but an act of graciousness. I find my greatest source of motivation is through divine intervention. Without courage and faith, your decisions to make a change is less likely to happen. Many of us get comfortable with our current situation even though we crave a better life full of wealth and freedom to choose whatever we can afford.

However, we lack the courage to break the chain of contentment or we feel that there are limited resources to obtain the proper tools to move forward with our aspirations, so we settle for what we already have rather than take a plunge into uncertainty and reach for more of what our purpose has in store.

It took a life-altering testimony to wake me up from being stagnant and complacent to a sense of urgency and becoming more deliberate. I surrendered to the call to take advantage of the opportunity, and I took a giant *leap of faith*.

If it feels right in the heart, then have no fear, just go ahead and jump. Let your conscience be your guide, you never know, normal life can change right before your eyes.

Folks, there is something wicked in the air that is making it hard for me to—

Breathe—in these global times of
unprecedented feasts and famine.
I too have been impacted by the pandemic
outbreak called COVID-19,
Resulting in a sense of poverty and
metaphorical emotional anxiety,
I starve from a financial setback…most importantly,
I suffer from fear of the unknown…how complex can it be,
Even though my spiritual faith is unwavering as
I face a multiplex of enemies seen and unseen from
cyberattacks to steal my personal identity,
And belittle me through radical discriminatory ideology,
And then, this epic coronavirus *Pandemonium*
(2020) effect, What the heck!
It ain't easy being me,
a man with color, integrity, and of dignity,
Dear, Lord! I'm in this new world of change
and social abnormal reality,
I look forward to a more minimalistic approach to life,
A less digitally driven…life,
an all-inclusive sisterly to brotherly love, no stress, no strife,
Again I just want room to—*breathe*.

It is easy to take life and our natural resources for granted or even forget the simple things that bring us so much joy. As a kid growing up, I remember my mother would start preparing food for dinner, and I would get in her way of things so she used to say, "Boy, go outside and play somewhere," and so I did. I would go out and play with the other kids in the drug-infested parks and playgrounds.

When violence and gunshots rang out, I would venture out deep into the woods and creeks not too far from our neighborhood. In those moments, I gained a true obsession with nature.

We were very fortunate to live in Saint Louis, Missouri, near central of the United States, a place where you get to experience all four seasons of sometimes extreme weather conditions.

I remember in the winter months my friends and I would wait until a blizzard calms down so we could go sledding, build igloos, make all kinds of snow angels, and have some hilarious snowball fights. Another thing we loved was riding on ski lifts to see some of the clearest and most colorful skies. I would look forward to going walking in a winter wonderland.

I remember the spring season; it seems like everything comes back to life. Animals would come out of hibernation, birds would sing melodic songs all day and all night, squirrels would like to play hide and seek and swing from tree to tree, the dogs would become rambunctious while chasing the cats and vice versa, invigorating showers would create a blooming medley of trees, bushes, and flowers with refreshing aromas. I used to, and I still do, enjoy spending time in a botanical garden because it gives me a feeling of being close to nature's paradise.

The summer season, well, we all have special memories and testimonies we can share. I can go on and on with the summertime madness, so I will just speak about some benefits. For the mind, body, and soul, you should travel around the world to experience different cultures to try their organic nutrients, exotic healing herbs, and spices.

You should make it your life's goal to visit as many natural international landscapes, beaches, geysers, waterfalls, mountains, caverns, swamps, lagoons, bays, and ravines nature has to offer starting with the Seven Wonders of the World, then visit thousands more.

My favorite season of them all is autumn. I can't get enough of the great outdoors. It encompasses my most memorable pastimes to include road trips along the picturesque Skyline Drive in Shenandoah, Virginia, to view what I call the "painted forest," a must-see fall-foliage spectacle.

I also enjoy overnight camping, fishing for Maryland blue crabs and striped bass locally known as rockfish out of the Chesapeake Bay (the world's finest estuary and wildlife habitat), roasting s'mores over a warm and cozy firepit with candid conversations with dear friends, grilling half-smoke hotdogs and Jamaican jerk chicken, and picking apples and pumpkins from a farm.

Another thing I remember is going to wine-tasting festivals at vineyards all across the country. Back to the words Asase Ye Duru, it is the meaning of the adinkra symbol, a language used by the Akan and Ashanti cultures out of Ghana, Africa, which means divinity of mother earth. Earth has no weight.

When I see that nature lover's symbol, I become engulfed with *nostalgia* as I envision reflections of a sun-kissed forest in the morning dew with symbols of love, growth, strength, and perpetual molecules that give us *life*.

I was once told to *take care of earth and she will take care of you.*

Good bye for now and stay blessed!

CPSIA information can be obtained
at www.ICGtesting.com
Printed in the USA
BVHW020801070322
630813BV00005B/198